Mexico

by Shirley W. Gray

Content Adviser: Professor Sherry L. Field,
Department of Social Science Education, College of Education,
The University of Georgia

Reading Adviser: Dr. Linda D. Labbo,
Department of Reading Education, College of Education,
The University of Georgia

COMPASS POINT BOOKS

Minneapolis, Minnesota

Compass Point Books
3722 West 50th Street, #115
Minneapolis, MN 55410

Visit Compass Point Books on the Internet at *www.compasspointbooks.com* or e-mail your request
to *custserv@compasspointbooks.com*

Photographs ©: Photophile, cover; Photophile/Bachmann, 4; Visuals Unlimited/McCutcheon, 6; Photophile/Jeff Greenberg,
7; Mark Harvey, 8; Visuals Unlimited/Ken Lucas, 9; Visuals Unlimited/Jim Merli, 10; Manfred Gottschalk/Tom Stack and
Associates, 11; Photri-Microstock, 12; Photophile/Jeff Greenberg, 13; Visuals Unlimited/Science VA, 14; Visuals Unlimited/Joe
McDonald, 15; Index Stock Imagery/Bruce Clarke, 16; Hugh Clark/Frank Lane Picture Agency/Corbis, 17; Robert Fried/Tom
Stack and Associates, 18; Root Resources/Shirley Hodge, 19; North Wind Picture Archives, 20; Archivo Iconografico
S.A./Corbis, 21; North Wind Picture Archives, 22; North Wind Picture Archives, 23; David L. Brown/Tom Stack and Associates,
24; North Wind Picture Archives, 25 top and bottom, 26; Archivo Iconografico S.A./Corbis, 27; Photophile/Bachmann, 28;
North Wind Picture Archives, 29; International Stock/Jeff Greenberg, 30; Unicorn Stock Photos/Jeff Greenberg, 31 top; Reuters
New Media/Corbiss, 31 bottom; Index Stock Imagery, 32; Photophile/Gordon Menzie, 33; Photophile, 34; Photophile/Jeff
Greenberg, 35; Visuals Unlimited/Audrey Gibson, 36; Photri-Microstock, 38, 39; Carl Schneider/FPG International, 40;
SportsChrome/Ron Wyatt, 41; Photophile/Bachmann, 42; Unicorn Stock Photos/Jim Shippee, 45.

Editors: E. Russell Primm and Emily J. Dolbear
Photo Researcher: Svetlana Zhurkina
Photo Selector: Dawn Friedman
Design: Bradfordesign, Inc.
Cartography: XNR Productions, Inc.

Library of Congress Cataloging-in-Publication Data
Gray, Shirley W.
  Mexico / by Shirley W. Gray.
    p. cm. — (First reports)
  Includes bibliographical references and index.
  Summary: An introduction to the geography, history, culture, and people of Mexico.
  ISBN 0-7565-0031-1
    1. Mexico—Juvenile literature. [1. Mexico.] I. Title. II. Series.
  F1208.5 .G73 2000
  972—dc21   00-008527

Table of Contents

"Hola!"

"*Hola*! Hello! Welcome to Mexico!"

You might hear this greeting if you visit Mexico. Mexico lies just south of the United States. It is a very long country. Its coastline along the Pacific Ocean stretches more than 6,320 miles (10,170 kilometers).

▲ *A Mexican dancer in native costume*

▲ Map of Mexico

The Rio Grande forms Mexico's northern border
with the United States. In the south, Mexico touches
two countries, Guatemala and Belize. Mexico is made

up of thirty-one states and a federal district. Its capital is Mexico City. With almost 10 million people, Mexico City is one of the largest cities in the world.

▲ Downtown Mexico City

Desert Animals and Plants

Mexico City and many other cities in Mexico are on a high **plateau** called the Central Plateau. The Central Plateau spreads up the middle of Mexico, from the south to the north. It actually ends in the United States.

▲ *Herding goats*

Most of the plateau is a desert area. Farmers grow crops here, but they can't count on the rainy season bringing rain. Many farmers **irrigate** their fields. They bring water to the fields through pipes or ditches. Corn, or maize, is the biggest crop grown in the Central Plateau.

▲ *An irrigated bean field*

Animals and plants in the Central Plateau can live without much rain. Cactus and yucca are the most common plants. They can live without rain because they store water in their thick leaves or roots. Almost 1,000 kinds of cactus grow in Mexico. One kind, the saguaro, grows to be as tall as a tree.

◀ *A beaked yucca*

Many reptiles live in the Mexican deserts. Gila monsters are poisonous lizards. They live under rocks during the heat of the day. The longnose snake hunts lizards and other snakes at night. Another reptile, a large lizard called the iguana, is active during the day and

▲ *A Gila monster*

sleeps at night. Iguanas have comblike rows of scales down their backs. Some people even keep iguanas as pets!

Mountains and Volcanoes

▲ *The Sierra Madre*

Mountains rise on both sides of the Central Plateau. The Sierra Madre Oriental towers over the eastern edge of the plateau. The Sierra Madre Occidental is on the west. A third group of mountains called the Sierra Madre Del Sur rises in the south.

Many of these mountains are actually volcanoes, and they are thousands of years old. One of the youngest volcanoes is Paricutin. It erupted in a cornfield in 1943 and quickly grew into a large mountain. The last time a volcano erupted in Mexico was in 1982.

▲ *Paricutin erupting*

▲ *The crater on top of Popoccatepl*

Rain falls regularly in the mountain ranges, so
many plants and animals live here. Pine, fir, and oak

▲ *Forest-covered mountains near Mazatlan*

forests cover the mountain slopes. Powerful wild-cats, such as ocelots, jaguars, and pumas, are found here.

▲ *An ocelot*

Rain Forests

The Yucatán Peninsula juts into the Gulf of Mexico in the south. A **peninsula** is a piece of land that is nearly surrounded by water. Tropical rain forests cover part of the Yucatán Peninsula.

▲ *The city of Cancun on the Yucatán Channel*

▲ *A macaw*

About 700 kinds of birds live in these rain forests. That's more kinds of birds than are in the United States and Canada put together. But the numbers of some birds that live in the rain forest are dropping. There are fewer parrots and macaws now. That's why it is against the law in Mexico to catch these beautiful birds.

The Ancient People of Mexico

The first people to live in Mexico may have come from Asia. Native Americans lived in Mexico for thousands of years before the Europeans arrived. They grew corn, built large buildings, and lived in cities. They also fought with one another.

Starting in the year 250, the Maya people thrived in Mexico. They lived on the Yucatán Peninsula

▲ Chichen Itza, the sacred city of the ancient Maya

▲ *An ancient Mayan sculpture*

for more than 600 years. Like many ancient people, the Maya prayed to many gods. They called the sun "our father" and the moon "our mother." They studied the movements of the stars and the planets and left valuable information for today's scientists.

The Maya people disappeared from Mexico around the year 850. No one knows what happened to them. Other Native Americans built cities on the Maya land.

The Aztec People

▲ *An Aztec sculpture of a human sacrifice to the sun god*

Several hundred years later, Native Americans called the Aztec lived in caves in north Mexico. Like the Maya, they prayed to many different gods.

According to a popular story, a god called Huitzilopóchtli told the Aztec to leave the caves. He said they should look for an eagle sitting on a cactus and eating a snake. This would be a sign that the Aztec had found a new place to live. For more than 100 years, the Aztec traveled through the deserts and

▲ *Ancient Aztecs living in caves*

over the mountains. Finally they stopped on an island in the middle of a lake. Then they saw an eagle sitting on a cactus. It had a long snake in its beak. The Aztec had found their new home.

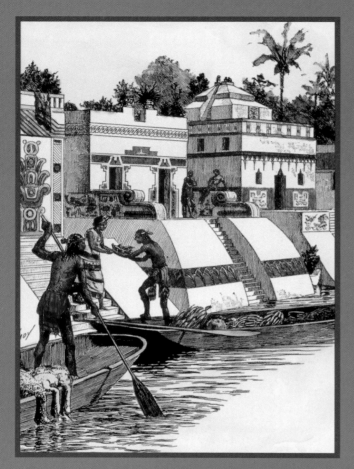

▲ *The canal in Tenochtítlan*

In the 1300s, the Aztec built a city on that island and called it Tenochtítlan. They built bridges to connect the city to the mainland. The water helped protect the city. This city stood where Mexico City is today.

The Aztec built pyramids to honor their gods. The Aztec believed that the gods were often angry. They believed they had to kill people to keep their gods happy. The Aztec also fought other groups and took their land.

▲ *Montezuma*

In the year 1502, a **warrior** named Montezuma became emperor of the Aztec. The Aztec soon

▲ *The Aztecs built the Pyramid of the Sun, the world's third largest pyramid.*

became the most powerful people in the area. Then a group of strangers arrived on the shores of their empire. They were explorers from Europe.

The Spanish Explorers

In 1519, an explorer from Spain named Hernando Cortés landed on the coast of Mexico. He had heard of a city built of gold. He and his men wanted the gold.

▲ Hernando Cortés

▲ Cortés meeting Montezuma

At first the Aztec thought Cortés and his men were gods. Soon they realized that the Spaniards had come to steal their gold.

Over the next year, other explorers from Spain arrived on the coast and joined Cortés's army. In 1521, the Spaniards attacked the city of Tenochtítlan. Thousands of Aztec and Spaniards died in that battle. Many beautiful buildings in the city were destroyed. Finally, Cortés defeated the warrior Montezuma. The Spaniards took over the Aztec Empire and called it New Spain.

▲ The Spanish army attacks the Aztecs.

Independence for Mexico

▲ *An early map of New Spain*

For the next 300 years, the Spaniards explored Mexico and settled there. Although Spain was very far away, the king and queen of Spain ruled Mexico. Most people in Spain were Roman Catholics, so Catholic priests moved to New Spain too. The

Catholic Church became the main religion in this area. Even today, most Mexicans are Catholic.

▲ *A Catholic church in San Miguel*

▲ *Native American slaves working in Spanish mines*

The Native Americans continued to live here too. The Spaniards made many of them slaves. Others died of European diseases or overwork. In time, some learned to live with the Spaniards.

In the 1800s, the people decided they did not want Spain to rule them anymore. In 1810, they fought against armies sent by Spain and declared themselves free. They formed the modern country of Mexico. Later, in the Mexican War (1846–1848), Mexico lost a lot of its land to the United States. Much of this land is today's state of Texas.

Mexico Today

▲ *A Mayan woman and her baby at home in Chetumal*

More than 98 million people live in Mexico today. Some are Native Americans, but most are of mixed Spanish and Native American descent. These people are called **mestizos**.

About one third of the Mexican people are Indians. The Native American people tend to live in certain areas of Mexico. One such area is in the state of Chiapas. This state is in the south near Guatemala.

▲ Mestizo young men in Guanajuato

▼ Mexican president Vincente Fox

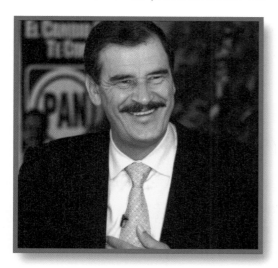

The head of the government of Mexico is the president. He or she is elected by the people. The president must be born in Mexico. Anyone who is eighteen or older may vote.

Mexico's flag and coat of arms are reminders of the Aztec Empire. Each has a picture of an eagle sitting on a cactus with a snake in its beak.

Most Europeans who settled in Mexico and other countries in Central America spoke languages that came from an old language called Latin. For that reason, this part of the world is called Latin America. The official language of Mexico is Spanish.

▲ *A stop sign in Mexico*

Some older Mexicans and Indians in remote areas still speak native Indian languages. The three most common Indian languages are Mayan, Náhuatl, and Zapotec.

Eating in Mexico

Like their neighbors in the United States, Mexicans eat many different foods. Families usually eat their main meal of the day after school, around 3 P.M.

▲ A Mexican meal

Corn is an important part of any meal in Mexico. Traditional Mexican meals include tortillas, thin pan-cakes made of coarse cornmeal. Tortillas are filled with meat, cheese, or beans and folded or rolled. Some popular tortilla dishes are tacos, enchiladas, and quesadillas.

▲ A woman making tortillas

Mexicans also cook with beans, rice, tomatoes, meat or fish, and peppers. Not all Mexican peppers are spicy hot, though. Some peppers are sweet and mild.

▲ A sidewalk vendor cuts pork for tacos.

Fiesta Time

Mexicans celebrate a holiday by having a party, or **fiesta**. One important national fiesta is *Cinco de*

▲ *A float in a Cinco de Mayo parade*

Mayo (Fifth of May). This celebration honors the battle in which the Mexicans fought the Spaniards for their freedom.

Another special day is *El dia de los Muertos* (Day of the Dead). This celebration, held on November 2, honors the spirits of the dead. Families go together to cemeteries and visit the graves of relatives. This is not a sad holiday, however. It is a time to remember and be cheerful. Often, families will picnic in the cemeteries and sing the favorite songs of their departed family members.

Most Mexicans also celebrate the Christian holiday of Christmas with several fiestas. Plays that tell the story of Mary and Joseph traveling to Bethlehem are held each night for the nine days before Christmas.

Then, the children break **piñatas** suspended from the ceiling. A piñata is a papier-mâché animal filled with candy and small toys. The children are blind-

folded and take turns swinging at the piñata with sticks. When the piñata finally breaks, everyone scrambles to pick up the treats that fall to the ground.

Music is an important part of life in Mexico. One popular kind of Mexican music

◄ A boy tries to break a piñata.

is played by the mariachi bands. The musicians in a mariachi band stroll through restaurants and plazas, singing and playing violins, horns, and guitars. Around the world, people think of Mexico when they hear a mariachi band.

▲ *A mariachi band with a traditional dancer*

Sports and Fun

▲ Mexican boys playing soccer

As in many other countries in Latin America, soccer is the most popular sport in Mexico. Children play soccer at school and at home. Mexico has several professional soccer leagues, and fans love to cheer for their favorite team.

Baseball is also a favorite sport. Baseball has professional leagues too. Some Mexican athletes have moved to the United States to play for American baseball teams.

▲ *Mexican athlete Fernando Valenzuela played for the Los Angeles Dodgers.*

▲ *Tourists visit the Mayan ruins at Tulum.*

People from other lands enjoy coming to Mexico. And tourism is important to the nation. Tourists travel to Mexico to enjoy its beaches, learn about its rain forests, visit Mexico City, and see the remains of the great Maya and Aztec cities.

If you visit Mexico, you will learn more about this special country. Then as you leave, you might say, "*Gracias*! Thank you! I enjoyed my visit to Mexico."

Glossary

fiesta—a celebration; a religious holiday

irrigate—to bring water to crops through pipes or ditches

mestizos—people of mixed Spanish and Native American descent

peninsula—a piece of land that is nearly surrounded by water

piñata—a papier-mâché animal filled with candy and small toys

plateau—an area of high, flat land

warrior—a soldier

Did You Know?

- Mexico City has the world's highest levels of air pollution.

- Mexico has the richest silver mines in the world.

- The first Mexican to win the Nobel Prize for literature was poet Octavio Paz. He won in 1990.

- Per person, Mexicans are the world's biggest soda drinkers.

At a Glance

Official name: *Estados Unidos Mexicanos* (United Mexican States)

Capital: Mexico City

Official language: Spanish

National song: *"Himno Nacional de México"* ("National Anthem of Mexico")

Area: 756,066 square miles (1,958,201 square kilometers)

Highest point: Pico de Orizaba (also called Citlaltépetl), 18,410 feet (5,610 meters) above sea level

Lowest point: Near Mexical, 33 feet (10 meters) below sea level

Population: 98,766,000 (1998 estimate)

Money: New peso

Head of government: President

Important Dates

250	The Maya Empire thrives in Mexico.
850	The Maya disappear from Mexico.
1300s	The Aztec build a large city called Tenochtítlan.
1502	A warrior named Montezuma becomes emperor of the Aztec.
1519	Spanish explorer Hernando Cortés lands on the coast of Mexico.
1521	The Spaniards attack the city of Tenochtítlan.
1810	Mexico wins its freedom from Spain.
1848	Mexico loses much of its land to the United States in the Mexican War.
1943	The volcano Paricutin erupts.

Want to Know More?

At the Library

Illsley, Linda. *Mexico*. Austin, Tex.: Raintree Steck-Vaughn, 1999.

Kent, Deborah. *Mexico: Rich in Spirit and Tradition*. New York: Benchmark Books, 1996.

Lasky, Kathryn, and Christopher G. Knight (photographer). *Days of the Dead*. New York: Hyperion Books for Children, 1994.

Stein, R. Conrad. *Mexico City*. Danbury, Conn.: Children's Press, 1996.

On the Web
Cinco de Mayo

http://latino.sscnet.ucla.edu/demo/cinco.html

For information about the history of this Mexican holiday

Mexico for Kids

http://explora.presidencia.gob.mx/index_kids.html

For a game-filled introduction, available in English and Spanish, to the music, stories, and government of Mexico

Through the Mail
Embassy of Mexico

1911 Pennsylvania Avenue

Washington, DC 20006

For information about the country

On the Road
Tourism Office of Mexico

1200 Northwest 78th Avenue

Miami, FL 33126

305/718-4091

To find out about visiting Mexico

Index

About the Author

Shirley W. Gray received her bachelor's degree in education from the University of Mississippi and her master's degree in technical writing from the University of Arkansas. She teaches writing and works as a scientific writer and editor. Shirley W. Gray lives with her husband and two sons in Little Rock, Arkansas.